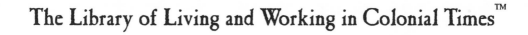

The Library of Living and Working in Colonial Times™

A Day in the Life of a Colonial Wigmaker

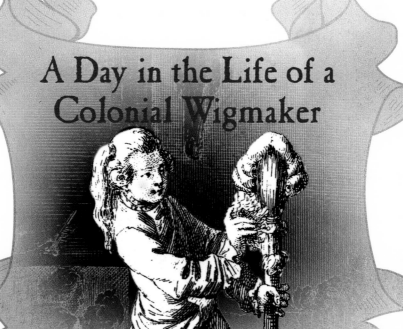

Kathy Wilmore

The Rosen Publishing Group's
PowerKids Press™
New York

To Bryan Brown, for the encouragement, humor, and grace that helped so much as I wrote this book—and to my mother, Julia C. Wilmore, who got me started.

Published in 2000 by The Rosen Publishing Group, Inc.
29 East 21st Street, New York, NY 10010

First Edition
Book design: Danielle Primiceri
Photo Credits: Cover, title p, pp. 15, 16, 19 © Stock Montage, Inc.; pp. 4, 7, 8, 12 © North Wind Picture Archives; p. 11 © The Granger Collection; p. 20 © Culver Pictures.

Wilmore, Kathy.
A day in the life of a Colonial wigmaker / Kathy Wilmore.
       p. cm. — (The library of living and working in Colonial times)
Includes index.
Summary: Discusses the fashion of wearing wigs in Colonial America, how wigs were made, and a wigmaker's role in the colonies.
ISBN 0-8239-5426-9 (lib. bdg. : alk. paper)
1. Wigs—United States—History—Colonial period, ca. 1600-1775—Juvenile literature. 2. Wigmakers—United States—History—Colonial period, ca. 1600-1775—Juvenile literature. [1. Wigs. 2. Wigmakers. 3. United States—Social life and customs—To 1775.] I. Title. II. Series.
TT975.W56 1999
646.7'248'097409032—dc21   99-11912
                                                                     CIP
                                                                      AC

Seth Hawkins, his shop, and the other characters in this book are fictional, but the details in this story about Colonial wigmakers and Colonial life are true.

Manufactured in the United States of America

Contents

Colonial America

Today, many fashions that are popular around the world are from America. During the early years of this country's history, fashions that were popular in America actually came from England and other parts of Europe.

From about 1607 until 1776, America was made up of different **colonies** that belonged to England. This period of time before the American Revolution is called Colonial America. During this time, wigs for men were one of the top fashions, and skilled wigmakers were important **craftsmen** of the day.

◀ *Boston, Massachusetts, was part of England's 13 American colonies.*

5

The Head Man

Seth Hawkins had been in the wigmaking business for many years. Like most Colonial wigmakers, he started as an **apprentice**, learning the craft from a master wigmaker. Then he spent years as a wigmaker's **journeyman**. He worked in a wigmaker's shop helping to train others.

Soon, Mr. Hawkins became the proud owner of his own shop. Many government officials, lawyers, and other important men worked nearby. Mr. Hawkins hoped that they would become his **customers**.

These court officials, like most men of the day, wore wigs. ▶

Time for a Shave

When a customer entered a wigmaker's shop, the shop owner greeted him with a bow. "What would the gentleman like today?" he asked. Some men only wanted shaves. Other men wanted new wigs.

Like many Colonial wigmakers, Mr. Hawkins was also a barber. The wigmaker's apprentice put a sheet around the customer's neck and brought hot water. Sometimes, the journeyman shaved the customer. If the customer was an important man in town, the wigmaker did the shaving himself.

◀ *A Colonial customer gets a shave.*

So Many to Choose From!

The windows of a Colonial wigmaker's shop had many different styles of wigs on **display**. Signs in the windows listed other styles. There were more than 100 different wig styles for men. Wigs came in many colors. White, black, brown, and gray were the most popular. Wigs of other colors, even blue, were also worn. The only hair color thought of as disagreeable was red.

The wigs were heavy, hot, and uncomfortable, but very popular. Almost every man who could afford it had at least one wig.

These are a few of the many wig styles of Colonial days. ▶

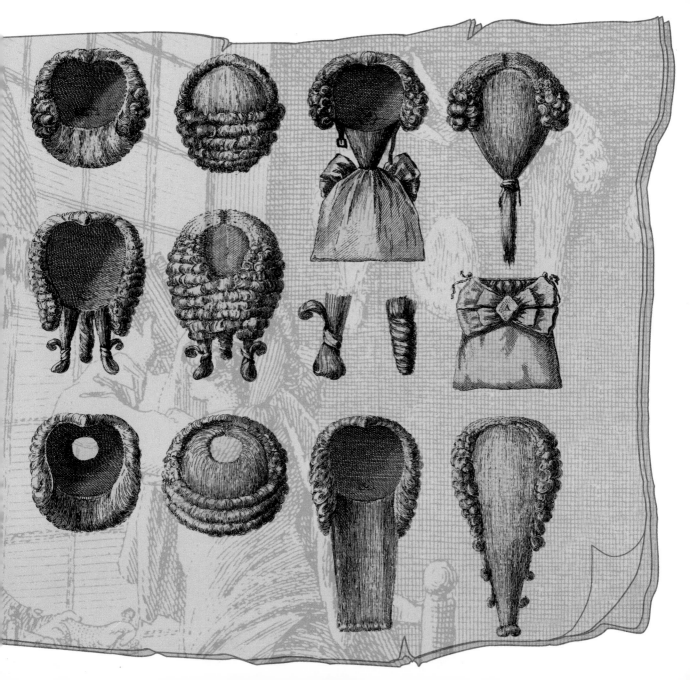

Measuring Up

A customer entered Mr. Hawkins's shop and told him that he wanted a new wig. The wigmaker and the customer looked at pictures and discussed styles while the journeyman shaved the man's head. Since most men wore wigs whenever they were in public, they shaved off all their real hair.

The wigmaker measured the man's head. He laid strips of paper across the man's head in different places. Then he made scissor snips in the paper to show how long each part of the **skullcap** should be.

◀ *This man is looking at popular wig styles worn by lawyers.*

Preparing the Hair

An apprentice prepared hair for the wigs. First, he sorted it by color, then tied it in **bundles**. He dusted each bundle with sand to soak up any oil in the hair. Then he shook out the sand and combed the hair. The shop's journeyman pinned the hair into curls. He boiled the hair for three hours, then put it in an oven to dry. (If he wasn't careful, it would burn!)

The wigmaker went through the prepared hair. He chose hair of the length and color the customer wanted.

This wigmaker gives a customer a shave while his assistant heats some curlers. ▶

By the Numbers

Mr. Hawkins used his measuring strips to make a **pattern** for the new wig. It showed him where each row of hair should go and how long each row should be. Then he wove hair together into rows of the proper length. For this wig, Mr. Hawkins used human hair knotted together with silk thread. Human-hair wigs were the finest and most expensive. (One wig would cost more than $250 in today's money.) Cheaper wigs were made of horsehair or goat's hair, silk threads, or other **materials**.

◀ *This woman is weaving hair for a wig.*

Stitching It Together

The journeyman made a headpiece for the wig. He started with a wig block, which was a dummy head on a post. He chose a dummy head that was the same size as the customer's head. Then he took a net made of tightly woven silk or cotton. He cut it to match the wigmaker's pattern. Then the journeyman sewed ribbon around the edges to hold the shape. When the skullcap was finished, Mr. Hawkins took the rows of hair he had made and **stitched** them into place, one row at a time.

This man is stitching hair into place. ▶

The Height of Fashion

When all the hair was sewn into place, the wigmaker inspected the wig. He trimmed any uneven places. He curled any **limp** places. At last, the wig was ready for the final step.

When the customer returned, Mr. Hawkins put the wig on the man's head. The apprentice handed the man a large paper cone to put over his face for protection. Then Mr. Hawkins sprinkled perfumed powder all over the man's head. The powder could be dyed any color a customer wanted, but this man wanted white.

◀ *Powdering the customer's wig was a last, special touch.*

Another Happy Customer

This man was pleased with his wig. He paid Mr. Hawkins the fee right away. Most wigmakers' customers paid fees once a year. The fee included care of the customer's wig throughout the year. Happy customers who told their friends about the shop meant more customers for Mr. Hawkins.

Web Sites:

Due to the changing nature of Internet links, PowerKids Press has developed an online list of Web sites related to the subject of this book. This site is updated regularly. Please use this link to access the list: www.powerkidslinks.com/llwct/dlcwig/

Glossary

apprentice (uh-PREN-tis) A young person learning a skill or trade.

bundles (BUN-dulz) Bunches or clumps of something fastened together.

colonies (KAH-luh-neez) Groups of people who leave their own country to settle in another land but still remain under the rule of their old country.

craftsmen (KRAFS-mun) Workers with special skills, especially those who work with their hands.

customers (KUS-tuh-merz) People who buy goods or services from someone else.

display (di-SPLAY) Show.

journeyman (JER-nee-man) A person who has learned a skill or trade and works for another person.

limp (LIMP) When something is loose, soft, or floppy.

materials (muh-TEER-ee-ulz) What something is made from or used for.

pattern (PA-tern) A shaped piece or a plan used as a guide when making something.

skullcap (SKUL-kap) A small cap that fits tightly on the head.

stitched (STITCHT) Sewed.

Index

BAKER & TAYLOR